D1504615

Grape Pruning: The Spur and Long Cane Systems Compared

Bulletin No. 160

by Iowa Agricultural Experiment Station

with an introduction by Roger Chambers

This work contains material that was originally published in 1915.

This publication is within the Public Domain.

This edition is reprinted for educational purposes
and in accordance with all applicable Federal Laws.

Introduction Copyright 2018 by Roger Chambers

COVER CREDITS

Front Cover
Szőlő metszés by Hirvenkürpa (Own work)
[CC BY-SA 3.0 - https://creativecommons.org/licenses/by-sa/3.0],
via Wikimedia Commons

Back Cover
More Grapes by Scott Bauer, *Agricultural Research Service / USDA*
Image Number K7248-1
[Public domain],
via Wikimedia Commons

Research / Resources
Wikimedia Commons
www.Commons.Wikimedia.org

Many thanks to all the incredible photographers, artists,
researchers, biographers, historians, and archivists who share
their great work via the Wikipedia family.

PLEASE NOTE :
As with all reprinted books of this age that are intended to perfectly reproduce the original edition,
considerable pains and effort had to be undertaken to correct fading and sometimes outright damage to
existing proofs of this title. At times, this task can be quite monumental, requiring an almost total
rebuilding of some pages from digital proofs of multiple copies. Despite this, imperfections still sometimes
exist in the final proof and may detract slightly from the visual appearance of the text.

DISCLAIMER :
Due to the age of this book, some methods or practices may have been deemed unsafe or
unacceptable in the interim years. In utilizing the information herein, you do so at your
own risk. We republish antiquarian books without judgment or revisionism, solely
for their historical and cultural importance, and for educational purposes.

Self Reliance Books

Get more historic titles on animal and stock breeding, gardening and old fashioned skills by visiting us at:

http://selfreliancebooks.blogspot.com/

introduction

Here at **Self-Reliance Books** we are dedicated to bringing you the best in *dusty-old-book-knowledge* to help you in your quest for self-sufficiency and food independence.

We're so pleased to bring you another title on Horticulture – this time a book on comparing different pruning methods for Grapes.

This special edition of **Grape Pruning : The Spur and Long Cane Systems Compared** was produced by the *Iowa Agricultural Experiment Station*, and first published in 1915, making it just over a century old. It is also known as **Bulletin No. 160**.

The book was written by T.J. Maney, who was the head of the *Pomology Subsection* of the *Iowa Agricultural Experiment Station*.

The book features sections on *Time for Pruning, Pruning Young Vines, Pruning the Second Year, Tying Up the Pruned Vines, Pruning and Its Relation to Insect Control*, and more.

A fantastic old book on the intricacies of Grape pruning. An essential read for all those new to Grape Culture and growing their first crop.

~ Roger Chambers

State of Jefferson, April 2018

GRAPE PRUNING
The Spur and Long Cane Systems Compared

BY T. J. MANEY

Grape pruning experiments carried on near Council Bluffs during the season of 1914 for a comparison of the "spur" with the "long cane and spur renewal" system, showed that the vines pruned after the long cane system yielded, on the average, 41 per cent more grapes than the spur pruned vines. These results indicate that the long cane system is of value for the southwestern and other sections of Iowa where grapes are grown. However, it must be recognized that these results are for one year only. Further experiment with the two systems must be carried on before the long cane system can be recomended unreservedly.

The pruning experiments grew out of a survey made by the pomology section of the Iowa Agricultural Experiment station in the summer of 1913 for the purpose of obtaining data relative to the methods of vineyard management in the vicinity of Council Bluffs. The one operation that attracted the most attention was the "spur" system of pruning which had been practiced here for a number of years. It is unlike the grape pruning systems that are used in the other grape growing regions of the United States and it was later decided to investigate it thoroughly.

This style of pruning is very well shown in fig. 1 which gives the impression that there is too much non-producing vine in comparison with the amount of bearing wood left for fruiting. In the case of this particular vine the lower wire of the trellis is not utilized at all for the support of fruiting canes.

This particular system of pruning perhaps had its origin in the fan type. The first grapes planted in this region were pruned according to the low-headed fan system. Each year the old canes were cut back to near the surface of the ground and the vine renewed by means of one year old canes which each fall were laid

---

Note: The various technical terms in this bulletin may be defined as follows:

Pruning: The operation of cutting off certain parts of the vine with the view of leaving only sufficient one year wood to produce the crop of fruit for the following season.

Training: The development and arrangement of the various parts of the vine on the trellis.

Spur Pruning: This is the type of pruning which is illustrated by the vine that is shown in fig. 1. It has been practiced largely in the vicinity of Council Bluffs, Iowa. All the fruiting wood in this type is cut back to two or three buds. These short canes or spurs are supposed to be distributed uniformly over the vine. In this type no additional provision is made for the production of renewal wood.

Long Cane Pruning: The type of pruning wherein a certain number of canes of the previous season's growth, consisting of eight or ten buds each, are left for the production of fruit during the following season. In addition to leaving the long canes, certain canes are also cut back to one or two buds in order to force a excess of plant food into the short spurs and thus cause their buds to throw out vigorous canes which can be used for fruiting wood the following season. The spurs are known as renewal spurs.

Fig. 1—A spur pruned vine which is in need of renovation.

down and covered with earth for winter protection. Later, by experience, the growers learned that laying down was unnecessary for the Moore's Early, Concord, Worden and Niagara, the varieties most extensively grown in this section.

The fact that it was unnecessary to bend the vines to the ground each year, influenced the growers to allow more of the older and stronger wood to remain on the trellis. In a short time the trellis became crowded with the old wood and as there was no room for long young canes, gradually the method of spurring took the place of the long cane renewal. So much of this old wood has now accumulated in the vines, as is shown by fig. 1, that they are badly in need of a thorough renovation to put new life and vigor into them. It is still possible to accomplish this object by the vigorous use of a saw and shears in cutting out the old arms and replacing them with vigorous young canes as is shown in the illustration on the cover page.

At the annual short course, which was held at Council Bluffs during January, 1914, the subject of grape pruning was discussed and the system wherein long canes and renewal spurs are used was demonstrated by the writer. Later in the spring the pomology section in co-operation with the Agricultural Extension department of the Iowa State College gave several pruning demonstrations in the vineyards near Council Bluffs. The result of this work was that a number of the growers were so favorably impressed with the new style of pruning that they offered parts of their vineyards to the Iowa Agricultural Experiment station for carrying out co-operative experiments in pruning.

EXPERIMENTS COMPARING THE SPUR WITH THE LONG CANE SYSTEM OF PRUNING

The pruning tests were carried out in the vineyards of J. W. Dorland, W. G. Rich, L. J. Johnson, Charles Konigmacher, and E. A. Hess.* Two rows of Concord grapes were selected in each of the first four vineyards mentioned. One row was pruned by the grower who followed the spur method. The other was pruned after the long cane method by the writer.

No particular system of training was followed on the old vines pruned by the long cane method except in a general way to direct the new growth toward the fan system. The main object was to prune according to the long cane system and at the same time reduce the amount of old vine, replacing the heavier wood with vigorous young canes and renewal spurs. The illustration on the cover page gives a very good idea of how the majority of old vines looked after the shears and saw had done their work. In contrast to this vine, the view in fig. 1 is representative of many of the spur pruned vines in the experiments.

During the growing season it was evident from the set and distribution of the fruit that the long pruned vines were going to give the highest yields. June 20, 1914, an inspection of the experiments was made by a large group of the grape growers and all were impressed with this fact. The fruit on the spur pruned vines was mostly bunched together along the top wire in a rather compact mass. Very few bunches were produced lower down on the vines.

In the spring of 1914 the bloom on the vines in all the vineyards was very abundant but heavy rains at blossoming time caused a poor set of fruit in many of the vineyards. The failure of the flowers to fertilize properly resulted in small and loosely formed bunches. The fruit produced was of good size and high quality. However, the yield was shortened considerably.

The grapes from the vines in both systems of pruning ripened at about the same time. The fruit was then picked and the weights recorded for the individual vines.

*Acknowledgment is gratefully made to these and other growers who so materially assisted in carrying on the experiments.

In all the experiments only the normal vines were considered in figuring the averages. In both the spur pruned and the long pruned rows some of the vines were not in a normal condition, being diseased, too young for bearing, or severely cut back, or, as with two of the vines, the grapes were not ripe at picking time.

The following tables give the records of the experiments in the different vineyards:

THE DORLAND VINEYARD TESTS

The vines in the Dorland vineyard were about 18 years old. A large amount of old wood had been accumulated on all the plants. This vineyard was the only one in which the vines were protected against disease and insects by the application of several sprayings with bordeaux mixture and lead arsenate. Black rot appeared on the leaves in July, but the dry weather prevented it from developing in all the vineyards. This was the first appearance of the disease since 1909. Insects were not numerous enough to be a disturbing factor.

TABLE I—PRUNING EXPERIMENTS—1914
Dorland Vineyard, Council Bluffs, Iowa.

Vine No.	Spur Pruning Yield in Lbs.	Long Cane Pruning Yield in Lbs.	Vine No.	Spur Pruning Yield in Lbs.	Long Cane Pruning Yield in Lbs.
1	6.50	4.00	16	11.25	10.00
2	5.50	5.00	17	8.00	12.50
3	4.50	6.00	18	6.75	12.50
4	9.75	10.00	19	4.50	11.50
5	6.50	7.00	20	9.75	12.50
6	12.00	10.00	21	8.00	8.75
7	7.50	17.50	22	10.25	19.00
8	11.75	12.50	23	4.50	12.50
9	11.75	15.00	24	2.25*	13.50
10	9.00	15.75	25	8.00	21.00
11	9.50	14.50	26	11.00	17.00
12	11.75	18.00	27	13.25	7.75
13	12.50	9.00	28	17.50	
14	8.00	17.00	29	10.00	
15	8.50	8.00	30	7.00	

*These vines were not normal in some respect and were not figured in the averages.

	Spur Pruning	Long Cane Pruning
Total number normal vines	29	27
Total production by normal vines	264.75 lbs.	318.75 lbs.
Average production per vine	9.12 lbs.	11.80 lbs.
Average percentage increase		28.2 %

THE RICH VINEYARD TESTS

The vines in the Rich vineyard varied from 12 to 30 years old. After Mr. Rich learned the long cane system he pruned the greater part of his vineyard according to this method in the spring of 1914. When he was called upon to prune one of the experimental rows according to the spur method, he found difficulty in again accustoming himself to the old style of spurring.

In consequence of this fact, many of the spurs were perhaps left longer than they would have been under strict adherence to the spur system.

TABLE II—PRUNING EXPERIMENTS—1914
Rich Vineyard, Council Bluffs, Iowa.

Vine No.	Spur Pruning Yield in Lbs.	Long Cane Pruning Yield in Lbs.	Vine No.	Spur Pruning Yield in Lbs.	Long Cane Pruning Yield in Lbs.
1	12.50	12.50	18	8.00	9.50
2	15.00	14.00	19	10.50	13.00
3	13.00	10.00	20	5.00*	19.00
4	10.50	15.00	21	10.00	15.25
5	10.00	15.25	22	8.50	14.50
6	8.00	12.00	23	16.50	11.75
7	12.00	10.50	24	8.25	15.00
8	14.00	12.75	25	11.00	11.00
9	11.50	14.75	26	5.75	14.50
10	10.37	13.50	27	11.50	17.00
11	10.00	14.00	28	11.25	16.00
12	15.00	6.12*	29	6.50	0.00*
13	11.00	14.50	30	11.25	12.00
14	11.00	14.00	31	11.50	11.50
15	9.50	24.75	32	14.50	12.50
16	14.50	14.25	33		20.25
17	13.50	16.00	34		12.00

*These vines were not normal in some respect and were not figured in the averages.

	Spur Pruning	Long Cane Pruning
Total number of normal vines	31	32
Total production by normal vines	346.37 lbs.	452.50 lbs.
Average production per vine	11.17 lbs.	14.14 lbs.
Average percentage increase		26.5 %

A small portion of the Rich vineyard was pruned during the autumn of 1913, before the long cane method was demonstrated to the Council Bluffs growers. The vines in this part were spurred very closely and were typical examples of the old style. The fruit was weighed from ten of these vines for comparison with other vines under experiment. Table III gives the results.

TABLE III

Vine No.	No. lbs. Produced	Vine No.	No. lbs. Produced
1	12.00	6	4.75
2	6.00	7	6.00
3	10.00	8	8.50
4	6.50	9	6.50
5	10.00	10	6.00
		Total	76.25

Average per vine	7.6 lbs.
Average per vine long cane pruning in same vineyard	14.14 lbs.

THE JOHNSON VINEYARD TESTS

The Johnson vineyard, consisting of about one thousand vines, was 4 years old. It was divided into two sections of 500 vines each. The south section was pruned by the spur method before the long system was demonstrated to Mr. Johnson. Later the north half was pruned according to the long cane system. In the experimental rows the long cane vines showed a decided increase over the spur pruned vines. This was also true of the whole north section, which in yield almost doubled that of the south part.

TABLE IV—PRUNING EXPERIMENTS—1914
Johnson Vineyard Council Bluffs, Iowa

Vine No.	Spur Pruning Yield in Lbs.	Long Cane Pruning Yield in Lbs.	Vine No.	Spur Pruning Yield in Lbs.	Long Cane Pruning Yield in Lbs.
1	7.00	14.50	18	6.75	9.00
2	6.50	12.50	19	6.50	0.00*
3	5.75	17.00	20	6.50	0.00*
4	3.75	12.00	21	9.75	0.00*
5	4.25	9.50	22	5.50	0.00*
6	0.00*	11.00	23	5.00	0.00*
7	6.75	11.50	24	4.00	12.75
8	4.25	12.00	25	6.75	11.00
9	5.00	9.00	26	5.75	15.25
10	5.75*	12.00	27	4.75	6.00*
11	8.00	13.75	28	7.75	14.50
12	0.00*	3.00*	29	8.00	11.50
13	0.00*	11.50	30	8.75	9.50
14	6.50	9.50	31	4.25	5.00
15	0.00*	8.50	32	6.50	
16	0.00*	9.50	33	5.00	
17	0.00*	10.00			

*These vines were not normal in some respect and were not figured in the averages.

	Spur Pruning	Long Cane Pruning
Total number of normal vines	26	24
Total production by normal vines	159.25 lbs.	272.25 lbs.
Average production per vine	6.12 lbs.	11.34 lbs.
Average percentage of increase		85.2%

THE KONIGMACHER VINEYARD TESTS

The Konigmacher vineyard was about 18 years old. Such a radical system of spur pruning had been practiced that the vines had accumulated a great mass of old wood on the lower parts, leaving only the portion of the vine on the upper wire for fruiting. In changing to the new system it was very difficult to obtain young canes for the lower wire. However, the vines under experiment were given a severe cutting back and the long cane system adhered to as closely as possible. To a person accustomed to using the spur system it would appear that the vines pruned according to the new way would be ruined. The same vines are now in better condition than any of the others in the vineyard and the fruiting records show the advantage which they gained in the first year over the spur pruned vines.

TABLE V—PRUNING EXPERIMENTS—1914
Konigmacher Vineyard, Council Bluffs, Iowa.

Vine No.	Spur Pruning Yield in Lbs.	Long Cane Pruning Yield in Lbs.	Vine No.	Spur Pruning Yield in Lbs.	Long Cane Pruning Yield in Lbs.
1	.50*	0.00*	20	6.00	6.50
2	6.50	5.50	21	4.00	23.50
3	11.00	13.00	22	8.00	7.00
4	.25*	10.50	23	1.25*	7.50
5	1.50*	5.00	24	3.00	0.00*
6	3.25*	2.00*	25	7.00	9.50
7	6.00	13.50	26	9.25	6.75
8	8.25	7.00	27	5.75	13.50
9	9.00	10.50	28	9.50	21.75
10	4.50	15.50	29	6.25	24.50
11	10.75	7.50	30	1.50*	10.00
12	6.50	11.50	31	17.75	14.75
13	2.00*	9.25	32	3.50	13.75
14	11.25	9.00	33	10.50	11.50
15	16.00	8.50	34	7.00	13.25
16	6.75	10.00	35	5.00	12.25
17	4.00	9.50	36	8.00	3.00*
18	9.00	2.50*	37	7.50	9.00
19	6.00	11.25			

*These vines were not normal in some respects and were not figured in the averages.

	Spur Pruning	Long Cane Pruning
Total number normal vines	30	32
Total production by normal vines	235 lbs.	362 lbs.
Average production per vine	7.83 lbs.	11.31 lbs.
Average percentage of increase		44.4%

TABLE VI—PRUNING EXPERIMENTS—1914
AVERAGE RESULTS
Dorland, Konigmacher, Rich and Johnson Vineyards

	Spur Pruning	Long Cane Pruning
Total number normal vines	116	115
Total production by normal vines	1005.37 lbs.	1405.50 lbs.
Total average production per vine	8.66 lbs.	12.22 lbs.
Total average percentage increase		41%

Observations were also made on the vineyard of E. A. Hess in which a large number of vines were pruned after the long cane system. However, no detailed records were kept on the production of these vines.

CONCLUSIONS

It is realized that too much dependence should not be placed on the results of one year's experiments. However, the fact remains that in the Dorland, Rich, Johnson and Konigmacher vineyards the production from the plots pruned on the long cane system average 41% higher than the plots pruned by the spur method. Such a showing indicates that the long cane system must have some good features. If it is to be of real value every grape grower should set aside a few vines and test the system for himself.

GRAPE PRUNING

To prune a grape vine intelligently the pruner necessarily must be acquainted with a few of the simple principles connected with the growth of the vine, viz.:

1. The fruit is produced on shoots which spring from the one year wood and therefore the pruning of the vine is primarily a renewal proposition. A certain amount of wood of the previous year's growth must be saved each year for fruit production and provision made to provide for a renewal growth which can be used the following year.

2. Generally speaking, operations which reduce the vigor of the vine tend to promote fruitfulness and factors which limit fruitfulness tend to promote vigor.

If too much of the new wood is left on the vine, overbearing results. On the other hand, if too little of the new wood is left, the vigor of the vine is directed to the production of woody growth. In this connection, bending, girdling or twisting the cane injures the tissues and causes a loss in vigor and an increase in fruiting capacity.

The best pruner is the one who takes consideration of these principles. Acting accordingly, he shapes and adjusts the main body of the vine to the training system which he has in mind as an ideal, and prunes the bearing part of the vine so that it will be renewed from year to year, never allowing the vine to overbear but making it bear to its full capacity.

PRUNING OLD VINES

The suggestions which are here given for pruning are applicable particularly to the conditions in southwestern Iowa. However, the same principles and type of pruning can be adapted with but a few exceptions to all parts of the state.

In southeastern Iowa, in localities where the soil is poor, less bearing wood must be used in order not to overtax the vigor of the vine. Black rot is also more prevalent in the eastern part of the state and in order to control this disease more easily, the canes sel cted must be arranged on the trellis so that good circulation of air will be insured.

Old vines which have been improperly pruned for a number of years present about the same pruning problems in all cases. The type of training already has been determined and the pruning merely becomes a matter of renovation. The old non-pro-

Fig. 2—The most productive fruiting shoots usually come from the buds in the middle portion of the fruiting cane.

ductive wood must be removed and one-year canes substituted for the production of fruit.

Where old vines have been spur pruned for a long number of years, as they have been in the Council Bluffs vineyards, they necessarily have acquired an excessive amount of non-bearing vine. The reason for this is because with the spur pruning no provision is made for renewal canes. With grapes the greatest growth takes place in the highest shoots and on the shoots farthest away from the main trunk. As a result, at pruning time, the highest shoots, being the strongest, are naturally selected for spurs. Year after year this selection is followed so it is not at all surprising that all the fruiting wood is on the top wire or that the side arms extend out eight to ten feet. These facts are well illustrated in fig. 1.

In changing from the spur system to the long canes with renewal spurs, the pruner must remember several things. The weakest fruit buds on a cane are the ones at the base and at the extreme tip, whereas the strongest are located six or eight buds out from the base. This statement may perhaps be disputed, but if actual observations are made of the long cane when in fruiting, it will be seen that the best bunches are on the shoots coming from the buds in the middle portion of the cane.

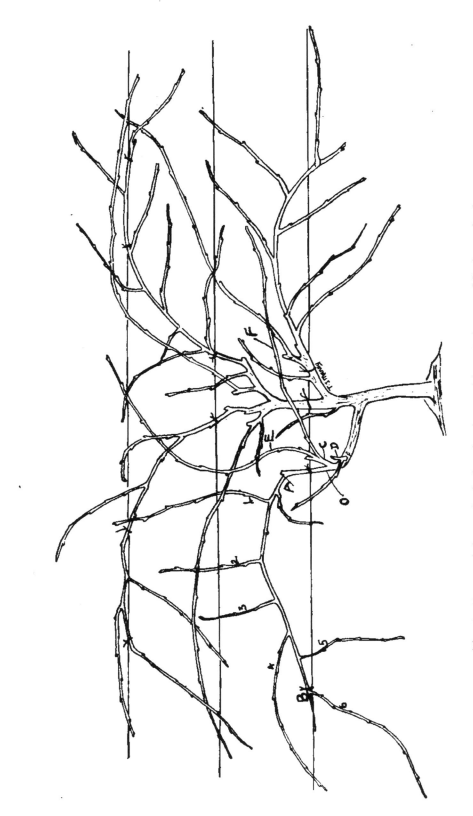

Fig. 3 - Unpruned fan trained vine showing position of the arm OB shown in fig. 4.

Fig. 2 shows this distribution of the fruit on one of the long canes.

With spur pruning it will be noticed that many of the spurs do not produce fruiting shoots, but on the contrary throw out heavy non-productive shoots which sometimes grow to a length of 20 feet or more. The reason for this growth is simple. The few buds at the base of the cane, which was spurred, were not fruit buds and consequently expended their vigor on wood growth.

The fact that the lower buds are not well adapted for fruit production is made use of in the long cane pruning. Long canes are selected for fruiting and others are cut back to two buds so that they will receive the extra food supply and produce strong woody growths.

DETAILS OF THE LONG CANE AND SPUR RENEWAL SYSTEM

The illustration on the cover page shows a vine which before pruning was very similar to the one shown in fig. 1.

The old wood has been cut out and its place taken by the long one-year canes. Renewal spurs of one or two buds have been left on the body of the vine.

The manner of pruning back an old vine is illustrated in figs. 3, 4 and 5. The part of the vine AO is an arm of old wood which was attached to the main body of the vine as illustrated in fig. 3. The pruning was done in the spring of 1914 and the cane AB was left as the fruiting cane. It produced the fruiting shoots $1, 2, 3, 4, 5,$ and 6 in the summer of 1914. In addition to leaving AB in 1914 two other canes were also cut back, forming the spurs C and D. Spur D did not develop a renewal cane but C produced two strong shoots, E and F, during the growing season. Fig. 5 shows the 1914 pruning of the part of the vine shown in fig. 4. The old part of the vine, OB, was removed entirely. Cane E was selected for the fruiting cane and D and F spurred to provide strong canes for the renewal of the fruiting wood in 1916.

Four to six such canes like E, having in all from 40 to 50 buds, together with replacing spurs, should be left on a vigorous vine. By following this system of pruning, it can be seen that the vine is kept in its proper location on the trellis.

With some of the older vines, it will be found necessary to replace the old vine completely. This can be done, and the production of fruit not reduced, by successive prunings extending over a period of three or four years. To replace the old vine a young shoot should be secured as near the ground as possible. This shoot must be trained according to the directions given for the pruning of young vines. While the young cane is being shaped the old vine can be cut out gradually. A period of four to five years is necessary to make the complete renovation. If young sprouts do not start readily from the base of the old stump, growth sometimes can be induced by slightly injuring the bark below the surface of the ground with a spade or some such tool.

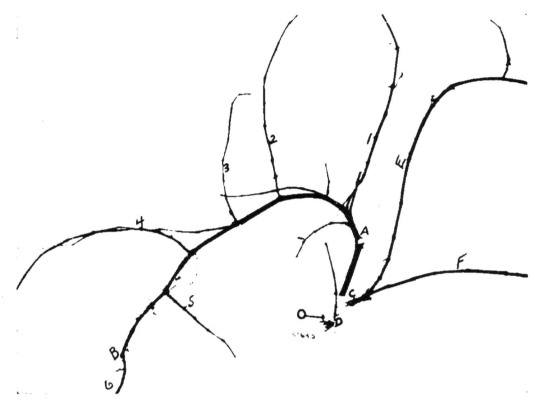

Fig. 4—Arm of fan shaped vine shown in fig. 3 before pruning. Attention is called to the vigorous canes produced by the renewal spur C.

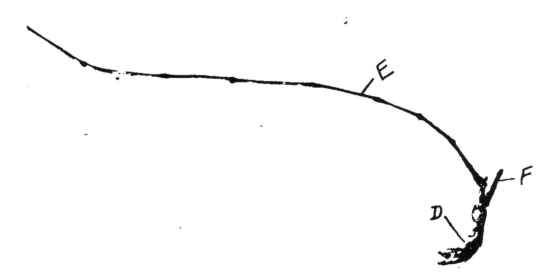

Fig. 5—Method of pruning the arm OB shown in fig. 4. Note the renewal spurs F and D.

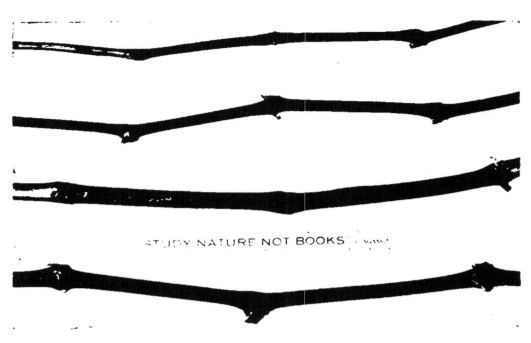

STUDY NATURE NOT BOOKS

Fig. 6—Medium sized short pointed canes with plump, rounded buds, produce the best fruit. The two lower canes are of the "bull cane" type. The buds on canes like these are usually wedge shape and are not very productive.

SELECTION OF FRUITING CANES

The production of fruit is much influenced by the type of fruiting cane which is selected by the pruner.

The best type of cane to choose for fruiting is one about the thickness of a lead pencil. The nodes on such a cane are short and the buds are round and plump. A cane of this type, having 10 to 12 such buds, is ideal for the long cane system. Some pruners are inclined to select the heavier canes with long nodes and wedge shaped buds. In fig. 6 canes of the short and long jointed types are shown.

The fact that a cane has made an unusual growth indicates that the formation of fruit buds has been sacrificed at the expense of wood growth. The Concord, and more particularly the Moore's Early grape, when planted on rich soil throw out a growth of heavy canes which are covered with short lateral shoots. In this case the heavy canes must of necessity be utilized. In doing so the average pruner will usually carefully clip off all the laterals, not realizing that some of the best fruit is often produced from these side shoots. The laterals should not be removed entirely but cut back to one or two buds as shown in fig. 7. The bud at the base of the lateral is not a good one for fruit production.

When a vine is found with an excessive wood growth, it is an indication of too much vigor. Such a vine may be given more

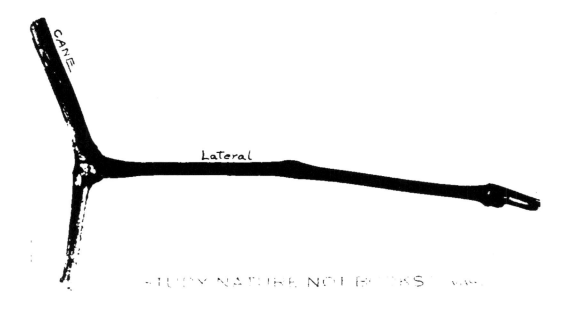

STUDY NATURE NOT BOOKS

Fig. 7—Often the best fruit is produced on the short laterals.

fruiting canes to use up the excess of plant food or the canes bent or twisted to induce fruit production. It is more profitable to raise grapes than useless wood.

TIME FOR PRUNING

Pruning of grapes can be started at any time after the wood has ripened up in the fall and before the sap starts flowing in the spring. If the vines are to be laid down for winter protection, the pruning should be done before the ground freezes. Perhaps, the spring is the best time to do the work from the fact that in some seasons parts of the vine are winter-killed and if these happen to be the canes which were pruned in the fall, it is impossible to replace them, whereas with the spring pruning it is nearly always possible to find on an unpruned vine a sufficient number of canes which have come through the winter uninjured. Pruning should not be done when the vines are in a frozen condition as the canes are then very brittle and easily broken off.

SUMMER PRUNING

Summer pruning is practiced considerably in the eastern part of this state, mostly, however, by growers who maintain the position that the bunches require sunlight for ripening. At Council Bluffs and in other parts of southwestern Iowa the vines make a very dense growth. Sometimes they are at least two feet across, yet the grapes ripen perfectly. Fig. 8 suggests how thick the growth becomes on the fertile loess soil. This vineyard produced over three tons of grapes to the acre. Only one picking was necessary as all the grapes ripened early and evenly. The only

Fig. 8—These vines received no summer pruning yet the fruit ripened perfectly.

summer pruning done was to remove the suckers from the base of the vine about the middle of July. Sometimes much damage is done by indiscriminate summer pruning, especially the kind where the pruner goes into the vineyard with a corn knife and proceeds to hack away at the young growth. The objection to this practice is that instead of diverting the energy of the vine into fruit production, the vine is apt to increase its growth activities by throwing out laterals which fill up the trellis, interfere with the circulation of air and tend to hinder rather than aid in the development of the fruit.

PRUNING YOUNG VINES

Grape vines as received from the nursery are either one or two years old. Many of the best growers prefer good one year plants. When planting the young vine, the growth is cut back to two eyes. Two or more shoots will start from these eyes and after they have made a growth of 6 to 12 inches all but the strongest shoot should be broken off. This throws the entire growth into the single shoot. Usually too little attention is given to the summer care of young vines. They are usually allowed to throw out a number of shoots, none of which makes sufficient growth to train to the trellis the second year. Vines which have made a weak growth the first year are benefited by again cutting them back to two buds the second season. This practice strengthens the root system and insures better canes for tying up to the first wire the third year.

PROVIDE TRELLIS AT END OF FIRST YEAR

At the end of the first year a trellis should be supplied. Oak or cedar posts set 18 to 20 feet apart should be used in the construction. The trellis should be strung with no. 11 galvanized wire. If two wires are used, the first is placed at 30 inches above the ground and the second about 26 inches above the first. Better training of the vine can be accomplished where three wires are used. In this arrangement the first wire is placed at 30 inches, the second at 43 inches and the third at 56 inches. The wires should not be fastened to the end posts by staples but should be wound on some sort of a simple reel. This simplifies the tightening of the wires, which is a necessary operation each season.

PRUNING THE SECOND YEAR

The pruning for the second year, provided the vine has made the proper growth, will be to head in the single cane and tie it in a vertical position to the first wire of the trellis. Early in the following growing season, the buds along the lower part of the stalk should be rubbed off and the growth thrown into the four or five upper ones which are allowed to remain in order to form the head.

THIRD PRUNING DETERMINES TYPE

The third pruning is the one which in a large measure determines the future type of training for the vine. There are a large number of different types of training, all of which have their good and bad features.

The one type which has naturally adapted itself to Iowa conditions is the fan system. With the proper distribution of the bearing wood, this type of training combines many of the features

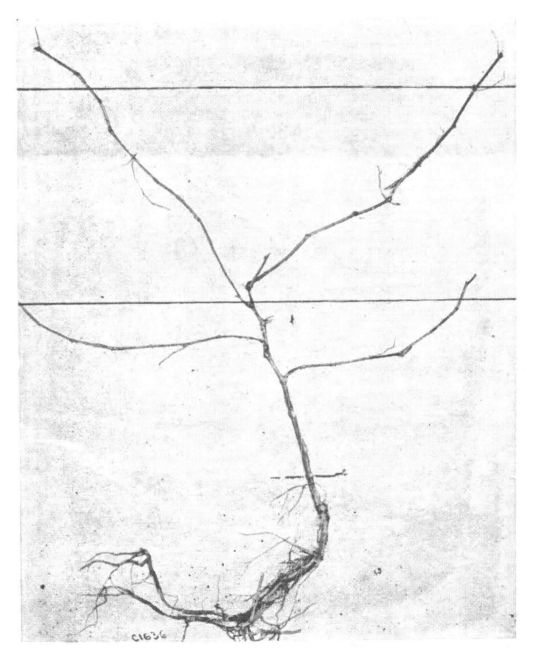

Fig. 9—Training a young vine to the fan system.

of the other styles and is peculiarly adapted to producing a large amount of grapes of good quality.

The pomology section is planning to carry on experiments in which the types of training now in practice in various sections will be tried out under Iowa conditions. A report on these will be made when data is obtained.

The fan system may be trained with a permanent single stem reaching to the first wire as is shown in figs. 9 and 11, or in regions where laying down is necessary the renewal canes may be started from a short stalk near the ground. Fig. 9 shows a three year old vine which has been pruned to make a single stem, high-headed, fan-shaped vine. Some fruit will be produced on the short arms during the third season. However, with the average young vine the wood should be headed back pretty severely so as not to permit the young vine to overbear.

After the fourth year, the pruning of the vine will be governed by the directions given in connection with figs. 3, 4 and 5.

By pruning to long canes each year and providing renewal spurs near their base, renewal is always possible and in addition, the arms of the vine are not lengthened out to crowd other vines on the same trellis.

PRUNING TOOLS

To do efficient work, the pruner must be equipped with the right kind of tools, the most important of which is the hand shears. There are many types of these on the market, some good and some wholly unsuited for fast work. The type of hand pruner shown in fig. 10, having a ratchet nut for tightening the blade, may be purchased at from $1.00 to $2.00. It does not pay to buy cheap pruners. Shears without the lock nut may be less expensive but they will continually give trouble by the nut working loose and thus permitting the blades to be sprung apart.

A pair of hand shears having a ratchet nut, together with a small keyhole saw, make an outfit which is efficient and easy to

Fig. 10—With tools like these the most efficient work can be done.

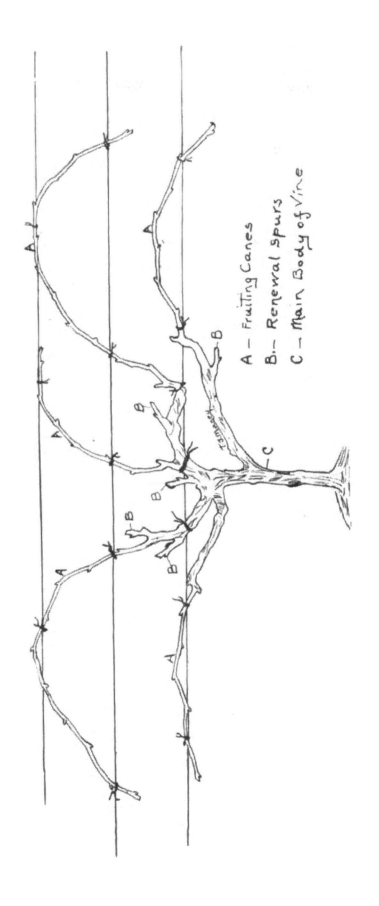

A — Fruiting Canes
B.— Renewal Spurs
C — Main Body of Vine

Fig. 11—Recurving the canes in tying usually tends to promote fruitfulness.

carry around. Wrapping the handles of the hand pruner with adhesive tape, or with leather from the top of an old shoe, gives the hand a better grip. Sometimes the heavy double pruners, or snagging shears, may be used to advantage. However, they are clumsy to carry. The keyhole saw will cut easier and can be carried in the pruner's pocket.

TYING UP THE PRUNED VINES

Tying up the canes after the pruning is finished is almost as important as the pruning itself. This work is usually performed by women and boys who know very little about the principles of pruning or training. Good pruning and ideals of training are often ruined by a poor tier. Whoever does the tying should be instructed in some of the principles of pruning.

The best material for fastening the canes to the wires is jute twine. In making the tie, the twine is first given a wrap around the wire and then tied about the cane. This prevents the cane from slipping on the wire or being injured by rubbing back and forth. The main body of the vine should be firmly secured to the wires. This is important because if the body of the vine is swayed by the wind, the canes when loaded with fruit and foliage will break as a result of the pressure.

In tying up a fan shaped vine to a three wire trellis, it is well to follow out the idea illustrated in fig. 11. The canes should be curved on the wires where possible. If the canes are tied in a vertical position the growth is thrown to the highest buds but if the cane is bent along the wire, or is recurved over the upper wire in umbrella style, and tied to a lower one, the mechanical injury caused by the bending tends to decrease the vigor of growth and consequently the energy is diverted into fruit production. Checking the growth by recurving the canes also tends to throw the growth vigor into the replacing spurs, which

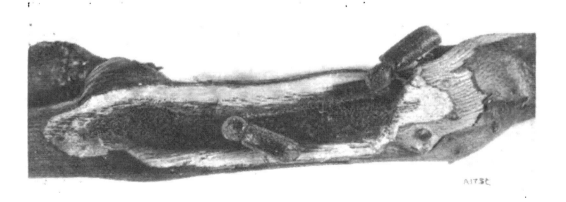

Fig. 12—The grape cane borer does serious damage but can be controlled easily by burning all the prunings.

is desirable from the standpoint of the production of renewal canes for the following year.

PRUNING AND ITS RELATION TO INSECT CONTROL

The grape cane borer (*Schistocerus hematus*, Fabr.) shown in fig. 12 has been very destructive in some of the vineyards in western Iowa. This little insect can be controlled best by pruning out all the infested canes and then burning all the prunings. It has been a common practice in the Council Bluffs vineyards to fill the soil washes with the grape prunings. These filled-in places have become breeding places for the borer and the injury from the insect in the vicinity of the wash usually is very severe.

In the practice of spur pruning the pruner usually neglects to remove many of the old spurs and thus provides an excellent breeding place for the beetles. When renovating an old vine, care should be taken to cut out all of these old stubs and burn them.

The grape cane borer is so easily controlled by burning the prunings that it should never be allowed to gain a foothold in the vineyard.

BIBLIOGRAPHY OF MORE IMPORTANT PUBLICATIONS ON GRAPE PRUNING

In the preparation of this bulletin a number of the more important publications on grape pruning were consulted. A partial list follows:

Alwood, W. B.,
    1893, Bul. Va Expt. Sta. 30.
    1898, Bul. Va. Expt. Sta. 94.
Bailey, L. H.,
    1893, American Grape Training.
    1914, Pruning Book, Fifteenth Edition.
Barry, P.,
    1883, The Fruit Garden.
Bioletti, F. T.,
    1897, Bul. Cal. Expt. Sta. 119.
    1907, Bul. Cal. Expt. Sta. 193.
    1914, Bul. Cal. Expt. Sta. 241.
    1914, Bul. Cal. Expt. Sta. 246.
Bush and Son and Meissner,
    1894, Catalog of American Grapes.
Card, F. W.,
    1895, Rep. Neb. Hort. Soc.
Dickens, A. and Greene, G. O.,
    1902, Bul. Kansas Expt. Sta. 110.
Fuller, Andrew S.,
    1894, The Grape Culturist, (Rev. Ed.)
Gladwin, F. E.,
    1911, Circ. N. Y. Expt. Sta. Geneva, 16.
Husmann, Geo.,
    1895, Am. Grape Growing and Wine Making, Fourth Edition.
    1911, Farmers' Bul. U. S. Dept. Agr. 471.

Keffer, C. A.,
    1893, Bul. Mo. Expt. Sta. 23.
    1906, Bul. Tenn. Expt. Sta. 77.
Lake, E. R.,
    1901, Bul. Ore. Expt. Sta. 66.
Lodeman, E. G.,
    1896, U. S. Dept. Agr. Year Book. 1896.
Mathews, C. W.,
    1901, Bul. Ky. Expt. Sta. 92.
Mohr, Frederick,
    1867, The Grape Vine. (Translation from German by Chas. Siedhof.
Munson, T. V.,
    1909, Foundations of American Grape Culture.
Paddock, Wendell,
    1898, Bul. N. Y. Expt. Sta. 151.
Quaintance, A. L.
    1901, An. Rept. Ga. Expt. Sta.
Ragan, W. H.,
    1902, Far. Bul. U. S. Dept. Agr. 156.
Revett, T. B.,
    1912, Bul. Ontario Dept. Agr. 202.
Starnes, H. N.,
    1895, Bul. Ga. Expt. Sta. 28.
Thomas, J. J.,
    1903, The American Fruit Culturist.